Alex Ferguson

Mike Wilson

Published in association with The Basic Skills Agency

Hodder & Stoughton
A MEMBER OF THE HODDER HEADLINE GROUP

Acknowledgements
Cover: Michael Melia/Retra

Photos: p 1 Julian Herbet/Allsport; p15 'PA' News Photo Library; p 3 George Douglas & Daniel Farson/Hulton Getty; p 11 Coloursport; p 20 Clive Brunskil/Allsport; p 26 Shaun Botterill/Allsport

Every effort has been made to trace copyright holders of material reproduced in this book. Any rights not acknowledged will be acknowledged in subsequent printings if notice is given to the publisher.

Orders: please contact Bookpoint Ltd, 39 Milton Park, Abingdon, Oxon OX14 4TD. Telephone (44) 01235 400414, Fax: (44) 01235 400454. Lines are open from 9.00–6.00, Monday to Saturday, with a 24-hour message answering service. Email address: orders@bookpoint.co.uk

British Library Cataloguing in Publication Data
A catalogue record for this title is available from The British Library

ISBN 0 340 80092 5

First published 2001
Impression number   10 9 8 7 6 5 4 3 2 1
Year   2007 2006 2005 2004 2003 2002 2001

Copyright © 2001 Mike Wilson

All rights reserved. No part of this publication may be reproduced or transmitted in any form or by any means, electronic or mechanical, including photocopying, recording, or any information storage and retrieval system, without permission in writing from the publisher or under licence from the Copyright Licensing Agency Limited. Further details of such licences (for reprographic reproduction) may be obtained from the Copyright Licensing Agency Limited, of 90 Tottenham Court Road, London W1P 9HE.

Typeset by SX Composing DTP, Rayleigh, Essex
Printed in Great Britain for Hodder & Stoughton Educational, a division of Hodder Headline Plc, 338 Euston Road, London NW1 3BH by Redwood Books, Trowbridge, Wiltshire.

Contents

Alex Ferguson is one of the most successful football managers of all time.

1 Introduction

In the spring of 1983,
Alex Ferguson led Aberdeen out
to play the mighty Bayern Munich.
It was the quarter final
of the European Cup Winners' Cup.
Aberdeen was not a team full of expensive stars,
just a lot of home-grown talent.

After an hour, the Germans were 2–1 up.
The manager had to do something – quickly.

He put on two subs.
He hoped they would turn the game around.
And they did.

A minute later,
one sub supplied the cross for the equaliser.
The other scored the winning goal
with minutes to go.
Aberdeen 3, Bayern Munich 2!

And that trick with the two subs . . .
He might try that again sometime . . .

2 Early life

On the last day of 1941,
Alexander Ferguson was born.
It was in Govan,
on the River Clyde, in Glasgow.

The world was at war.
The shipyards on the Clyde
were bombed at night
by German planes.

'Where I come from,' he said later,
'everyone relied on everyone else.
We had all seen hárd times
at some time or other.'

Alex's dad told him
you had to be honest and loyal.
You had to have drive.
You had to have faith in yourself.
You had to work hard.
And never give in. Never say die.
These were the keys to success.

Alex's dad worked in the shipyards in Clyde.

Alex's dad was also called Alex Ferguson.
He was a union man, a Labour voter.
He worked in the shipyards.
Alex's mum, Lizzie, worked in a factory.

His dad told Alex he had to learn a trade.
So at 16, he began to learn to be a toolmaker.
He stuck at it for the full five years.

And, just like his dad,
Alex was a shop steward in the union.
He liked being a leader.

One time, he took the men out on strike.
They won a pay rise.

But by then,
he knew that football was his future.
At 16, he was playing for Queen's Park.
(He was still at work.)

And he played for Scotland
as a schoolboy.

3 Ferguson the Player

Alex left the shipyards in 1962.
He went to play for St Johnstone,
then Dunfermline.

He played centre-forward.

Alex was not pure skill on the ball.
He didn't score class goals.
But he did score 97 goals in 145 games
for Dunfermline.

He had an eye for a goal.
He'd fight for every ball.
And he was strong.
He'd take the knocks.

The will to win was so strong.
He'd never say die.

4 Rangers

In 1963, Alex was spotted by Rangers.
He scored a hat-trick against them!
Rangers signed him in 1967.
For Alex, this was a dream come true.
Rangers had been his team
when he was a boy.
But the dream ended badly in 1969.
Rangers lost the Scottish Cup final to Celtic.

In the first minute, Celtic had a corner.
Alex forgot to mark his man.
Celtic scored with a free header.
Later, Alex missed an open goal.
In the end, Rangers lost 4–0.

After that, Alex's playing career went downhill.
His playing days were soon over.

All in all, Alex played for 16 seasons.
He scored 180 goals in 350 games.
But he never won the things he wanted to win.
That would have to wait
until he was a manager.

5 Ferguson the Manager

He got his first job as a manager in 1974.
It was at East Stirling.

Alex was there only four months.
But in that time,
you could see all the tell-tale signs
of Alex Ferguson the Manager.

East Stirling were stuck
down at the bottom of Division Two.

They had no money,
no good players, and no fans.
They hadn't won anything
since 1932.

Alex started to build the youth team.
He knew that was the key to success.

He was hard on his players.
He wanted them all to give 100%.
One player wanted to go to a wedding
one Saturday.
Alex said no. Football comes first.
The player went to the wedding,
so Alex banned him from playing.

He asked the Board for money
to buy new players.
They gave him all they had – £2,000.
Even back in 1974,
that was not a lot of money!

After four short months,
Alex moved – to St Mirren.
But by that time,
East Stirling were up in the top six.
Crowds were twice as big.

And they'd beaten big rivals Falkirk 2–0
in a local derby.

Ferguson the Manager was on his way!

6 Aberdeen

At St Mirren it was the same story.

In one season,
they went up to the First Division.
Two years later,
they went up to the Premier League.

But St Mirren were still only small fry.

At last, in 1978,
Alex was spotted by
a bigger club – Aberdeen.
They were a good side.
They were just behind Rangers and Celtic
at the top of Scottish football.

At first, the fans were not sure
about the new man.

He clashed with some of the players, too.

Some players went clubbing
after they'd lost a match.
Alex went mad.

One player had a new hair-do, a perm.
(Perms were in fashion at the time.)
Alex went mad.

Some players were partying
after drawing a match.
Alex went mad again.
'A draw is not good enough,'
he told them.
'You must have the will to win!'

It was a shaky start.
Yet the team came fourth
in the League that season.
And they got to the final
of the League Cup.

It was a sign of things to come.

The next season, 1979–80,
Aberdeen won the League.
And they did it in style.
They had a run of 15 games
without a loss.

Alex Ferguson's tactics helped Aberdeen to win the League
three times. Players had to give him 100%!

In Scotland, Aberdeen won everything
in the next six years.

The League three times.
The Scottish Cup four times.
The League Cup once.
The Dryborough Cup once.

But it was in Europe
that Alex Ferguson and Aberdeen
had the greatest glory.

It started with that famous win
against Bayern Munich in 1983.
But then they went on
to beat Real Madrid 2–1
in the Final.

(Alex put on a sub again.
The sub scored in extra time!)

The Real Madrid Manager said:
'Alex Ferguson's team
is not full of super-stars.
The team did not cost a fortune.
But they have what money can't buy.
They have team spirit.'

7 Scotland Manager

In 1985–86, Aberdeen
were at the height of their success.
But Alex was on the move again.
This time, he was Scotland Manager.

He had always wanted
to work with Jock Stein, the old Manager.
Alex has called it learning from a master.

But Jock Stein died suddenly.
It was at a Wales–Scotland match in 1985.

Scotland got through
to the 1986 World Cup in Mexico.
But they had no manager.
Alex was the obvious choice.

In Mexico, Scotland didn't do so well.
They lost two games, to Denmark and Germany.
They drew another 0–0 against Uruguay.
They were soon out of the World Cup.

And Alex was ready
to go back to club football.

8 Manchester United

In November 1986,
Man United were second from bottom
in the League.
The club had gone 19 years
without a major win.
They had spent millions
on big-name players.
And it had got them nowhere.

They offered Alex the job
of making Man United
a world-class club once more.
It was the one job that Alex wanted.

It was a big job.
It was a big club,
with a history of fame and success.
But Alex knew there were problems.

The players were slack, and unfit.
There was a drink problem.
Alex says it was like a social club,
not a football club.
And team spirit was low.

Alex Ferguson became the manager of Manchester United
in 1986.

He did the same at Man United
as he did at St Mirren and Aberdeen.
He built up the youth team.
Sold off some of the players.
Built a new team.
Worked on team spirit, and the will to win.
But it took time to turn things around.

In December 1990,
Man United were still struggling.
They were losing too many games.

In September,
Alex had the low point of his career:
United lost 5–1 to Manchester City.
People were saying Alex's job was on the line.

He was saved by a win in an FA Cup tie –
a 1–0 against Nottingham Forest.

Then United had four away matches
on the way to the Final.
They played Hereford United,
Newcastle United and Sheffield United.
Machester United also played
Oldham in the semi-final.

In the Final,
United beat Crystal Palace
1–0 in the replay.

At last, after nearly four years,
Alex had his first major win for United.

United's faith in Alex Ferguson
had finally paid off!
In the next few years,
Alex Ferguson's plans all worked out.

The scouts filled the youth team
with talent.
And that talent made it into the first team:
Ryan Giggs, Phil and Gary Neville,
David Beckham, Paul Scholes and Nicky Butt.

(Alex's own son, Darren,
also worked his way up
from youth team to first team.)

But Alex was in the market
to buy new players as well.
And he spent wisely.

Peter Schmeichel came from Denmark
for only £500,000.
Eric Cantona came from Leeds
for just £1 million.
Roy Keane came from Forest
for £3.75 million (then a club record).

Later, he added Andy Cole
to the squad, for £6 million.

Then he broke the records again:
he signed Dwight Yorke from Aston Villa,
for a record £12.5 million.
(In their first season together,
Yorke and Cole scored 53 goals!)

In 1999, Alex paid £10 million
for Dutch defender Jaap Stam.
Some said it was a lot of money
for a defender.
But Alex was clear:
Stam was one of the best in the country,
and a bargain.

With players like these,
how could Man United lose?

9 Glory Years

Alex Ferguson built a team
to take on the world.
English football was just too small for them.

Since 1990,
Man United have won
the League 6 times (and been runners-up three times),
the FA Cup 4 times (and been runners-up once),
the League Cup once (and been runners-up twice),
and the Charity Shield four times.

They won the Double in 1994 and 1996.

In Europe,
they won the European Cup Winners' Cup
and the European Super Cup in 1991.

Alex Ferguson celebrating Manchester United winning
the FA Carling Premiership in 2000.

The only trophy left to win
was the European Cup.

And in 1999 they did it in style!

On the way to the Final
they had to beat the best in Europe.

They beat Inter Milan 2–0.
They beat Juventus 3–2,
after being 2–0 down.

After those wins,
Alex knew he could win the Final.

They were playing Bayern Munich.
And Alex knew how to beat them.
He'd done it before –
with Aberdeen in 1983.

But even Alex Ferguson did not know
the drama there'd be in that match.

10 That Match

Alex has said:
'This team will always be remembered
for their last-minute goals.
For never giving in!'

And it's true – United always seem to score
just as the other team is getting tired.

Remember the two goals in two minutes
against Liverpool in the FA Cup fourth round?

Remember the equaliser
from Paul Scholes against Inter Milan?

Remember that last-minute goal
by Ryan Giggs against Juventus?
Or the great winner Giggs scored
against Arsenal in the FA Cup?
(Man United were down to 10 men.
Giggs ran 60 yards with the ball
to score the goal of the millennium!)

But nothing beats the two goals in two minutes
in the European Cup Final
against Bayern Munich.

That was Manchester United's finest hour.
And it showed why Alex Ferguson
is the best Manager in the world.

Man United were without some key players:
Roy Keane and Paul Scholes
were missing from midfield.

Then Man United went 1–0 down
after only six minutes.

To make things worse,
United didn't look like scoring.

But Alex Ferguson did not give up.
He knew his team could still win.

At half time, Alex made a speech.
'At the end of this match,' he said,
'you will all go up to get your medals.

'If the score stays 1–0,
you will get losers' medals.

The European Cup
will be six feet away from you.
And you won't be able to touch it.'
'Now go out there,' he said,
'and give 100%.
And don't show your face in here,
if you don't give 100%.'

That speech really did the trick!
In the second half,
the players were totally fired up!
But Alex's tactics played a part too.

In the second half,
Alex put on two subs:
Teddy Sheringham
and Ole Gunnar Solksjaer.

Sheringham made it 1–1
with 90 minutes played.
Just 60 seconds later,
Solksjaer flicked in the winner
from a Sheringham header.

Bayern Munich were on their knees.
They couldn't believe it.

Alex's old trick with the two subs
had worked again!

11 The Best Manager in the World

What makes Alex Ferguson
the best Manager in the world?

One player explains:
'He puts pressure on you
to do your best all the time.
He expects you
to have the mental strength to stand it.

If you repay him, he is very loyal.
But if you don't, he's not slow to tell you
you've let him down.
He's very honest.'

A manager needs to be able
to tell a player off.
(Some players used to call Ferguson
'the hair-drier'
because of the hot blast of his temper!)

But he also needs to know when to back off.
(Who else could have calmed Eric Cantona,
and got the best out of him?)

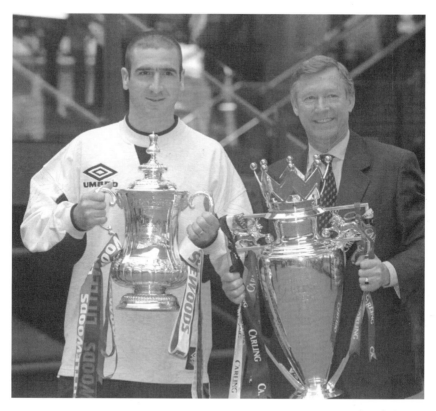

Eric Cantona was one of Manchester United's star players in 1996 when they won the FA Cup and the Premiership.

But what really makes Alex Ferguson the greatest
is this:
when United went 2–0 down
against Juventus in 1999,
Alex did not give up.
Giving up was out of the question.

He looked at his watch.
Only 11 minutes gone.
'Good,' he said to himself.
'Plenty of time left
to get three goals
and win the game.'

If the Manager thinks that way,
and gets his players to think that way,
they'll be the best team in the world!

12 Life Outside football?

Alex has a wife, Cathy,
and three sons:
Darren, Mark and Jason.

He likes horse racing,
and owns a horse called Queensland Star.
And he likes a game of golf now and then.

He has done some work for New Labour
and for the Scottish Labour Party.

But his only love is football.

He was made *Sir* Alex Ferguson
in January 2000.
He said it was not just an honour for him.
It was an honour for all his family and friends.
It was an honour for football.

It was an honour for Manchester United
and everyone who works there.